Returning Home

Worship Resources For Lent

Based On The Prodigal Son

David R. Mattson

CSS Publishing Company, Inc., Lima, Ohio

RETURNING HOME

ISBN 0-7880-1784-5   PRINTED IN U.S.A.

To Kimberly

Acknowledgments

A great deal of the inspiration for this book came while reading Henri Nouwen's wonderful book, *The Return of the Prodigal Son*. I found myself giving copies of this book as gifts and wishing my entire congregation could have the opportunity to read it. And not only read it, but actually to see and experience the overpowering work of Rembrandt that graces its cover. Certainly, inspiration also came from the wise words of German Lutheran pastor, Helmut Thielicke. He applies this wonderful story, not only to individuals, but also to all post-war Europe!

I thank the congregations I have served for encouraging this sort of variety in worship. King of Glory Lutheran Church, Fountain Valley, California for letting me loose to experiment with drama for the first time. Living Christ Community Church, Flagstaff, Arizona, who experienced the rough version of this book first-hand, enthusiastically ran with the scripts, and certainly improved on them in the process. I thank God for their creative energy. Gloria Dei Lutheran Church, Dana Point, California, for their invitation to begin again.

Like the elder son in the parable, I am always tempted to take-for-granted people who on a daily basis provide a home for me. And so, thank you — to my parents, Richard and Anna Mattson for living out the grace of the Father towards me; to my sisters and brothers who at times have physically lived the Prodigal Son story with me in a myriad of ways; and above all, I'm enriched daily by my wife Kimberly and our children Emma and Anders. It is easy to get lost in this world, in a variety of ways. They send out in a daily way a "homing signal" of God's mercy to me, a prodigal father and husband.

Table Of Contents

Introduction

"Truth is not nimble on its feet." The Danish philosopher Soren Kirkegaard meant by this statement that the truth of the Gospel is certainly saving, in and of itself, but it must be heard. The truth must be communicated in a way that is received. Sometimes communication breaks down because a life-changing hearing of a biblical story does not occur because of a casual familiarity.[1] That is certainly the case with the story of the Prodigal Son. It is perhaps the world's most familiar story. That is the wonder of preaching on the Prodigal Son and the great challenge.

By using the monologues, the sermons, the artwork, and the orders of service, *Returning Home* will, I hope, bring new insights, freshness, and vitality to your congregation. The Prodigal Son story is the timeless word of God's relentless love. When it is proclaimed with passion, it draws readers into identifying with one of the characters. The use of monologues brings home that identification even more intensely.

Notes On The Orders Of Service

Music: These abbreviations are used in the Orders of Service section: WOV — *With One Voice* hymnal; LBW — *Lutheran Book Of Worship* hymnal. The music that is suggested in each service complements the theme of each of the monologues. These hymns are simply suggestions and there are many other hymns and songs from other resources that could be easily substituted.

For Ash Wednesday and Good Friday, many congregations have long-standing traditions which cannot and should not be changed. The order of service that is included in *Returning Home* for Ash Wednesday is the imposition of ashes. For Good Friday, the service included is a Tenebrae service and includes the reading of the seven last words, a solo after each reading, and the stripping of the altar. The cross may be covered in black cloth. This may or may not be practical for your congregation, depending upon the layout of your sanctuary.

7

Optional Use Of Slides During The Worship Service

For the five Wednesday worship services, a slide of a famous painting on the Prodigal Son story may be used to enhance the message. There are at least four options in terms of using slides during the worship services:

1. Use of the Rembrandt painting: *The Return of the Prodigal Son*. This painting is to be found in many art history, art collections, and art appreciation books at your public library. Simply have a photographer take colored slides of this painting to be used for worship.

For example, in my parish we chose to use the Rembrandt painting. A photographer (nonprofessional) from our parish took colored slides of this painting from an art history book. He focused in on several different aspects of the painting for each service of worship:

Lent 1 — the slide was of the entire painting.
Lent 2 — the slide was of men in the background of the painting.
Lent 3 — the slide was of the father's face.
Lent 4 — the slide was of the father's hands.
Lent 5 — the slide was of the entire painting.

2. There are almost an unlimited number of famous paintings on the Prodigal Son story. A parish could choose to show a slide of a different painting each week to highlight a theme. You might also check with your local library, school district, or university to see if they already have slides on religious works that might be checked out.

3. Do not use slides at all. The services and the monologues stand on their own. Simply remove the introduction at the beginning of each order of service.

4. Be creative. Let your Sunday school department illustrate the front cover of the bulletin or have children draw on "write-on" slides to illustrate the monologues. Let an artist from your own

parish create a representation of the Prodigal Son story in whatever medium he or she chooses.

This series is easily adaptable. People learn and remember by using all of their senses. I have used three of the five senses — sight, sound, and touch. Certainly taste and smell could also be incorporated in some creative way.

Notes On The Monologues

The scripts were written to involve the laity in the service. A clergy person certainly can perform most of them, but this is an opportunity to involve a wider group of people from each parish. People who enjoy drama, can passionately express themselves, and can memorize scripts are most desirable. On a practical level, the more people that are involved in the monologues and the leadership of each service, overall attendance also seems to increase.

The monologues are most effective when they are memorized, but hand-held notes are also appropriate. A special note: if the mother of the prodigal chooses to read from behind the congregation or out of sight, then memorization is not needed but simply dramatic reading.

The costumes for each character are described at the top of each script. They are very simple and are easily attainable.

The props are also very simple, but they are very important in bringing out a certain theme for each character. This will become self-evident as you read through each script.

Lighting changes during the service enhance the overall effect of the monologues. A spotlight may or may not be used, but certainly turning off some of the lights to focus the congregation's attention on the actor is appropriate.

Returning Home Throughout The Church Year

The story of the Prodigal Son from Luke 15 does come up in the common lectionary on the Fourth Sunday in Lent (Year C). One of the monologues could certainly be used at that time.

Also, for those clergy who preach sermon series, *Returning Home* could certainly be used very effectively for that purpose.

9

This could easily be done during the summer months, during the Season of Pentecost when many congregations change from their regular routines.

A Final Note On *Returning Home*

German pastor Helmut Thielicke wrote, "We must read and hear this gospel story as it was really meant to be ... news that would stagger us if we were able to hear it for the first time as a message that everything about God is so completely different from what we thought or feared...."

My hope is that *Returning Home* will stagger the person who has heard and heard and heard the Prodigal Son story, so that he/she can no longer really hear it. By the power of the Spirit, may this story stagger us again, or at least cause a lump in the throat of inexpressible joy.[2]

Getting Lost At Home

Our theme for Lent is "Returning Home." Through dramatic first-person portrayals, artwork, and music, we will look at the Prodigal Son story in depth for the next forty days. I hope this series, *Returning Home*, is a wonderful preparation for your Easter celebration.

For my sermon tonight, I have three questions. The first question: *To whom do you relate in this story?*

When you hear the story of the Prodigal Son, you can't help but identify with one or more of the main characters. To whom do you relate in this great story?

Are you the wild younger son who wasted his father's money, practically his life, but received a second chance? Do you personally know something about second chances?

Or are you more like the older son? Industrious, practical, steady, reliable, but maybe with just a hint of jealousy, just a touch of feeling that you're taken for granted?

Or do you relate more to the father in the story? Maybe you have a child who has kept you up more than one sleepless night?

Or maybe you identify with all the major players? One day, you're the older brother, feeling left out and unappreciated. The next day, you're the prodigal son and the words of Saint Paul move from ancient history to personal autobiography: "The good I want to do, I do not do. The evil that I do not want to do, this is what I do. Who can help me!" And finally, the following day, you "live large" like the loving parent God calls all of us to be.

When you hear the story of the Prodigal Son, with whom do you identify most closely?

Back in the days of "fire and brimstone" preaching, a sermon on the Prodigal Son would have screamed about drunkenness, sexual immorality, and total depravity; many people, perhaps most, would sit back in their pew and breathe a sigh of relief, "Phew, at least the preacher's not speaking about me!"

11

My guess is that, because we are in church, because you have taken the time and energy to be here, most, if not all of us, whether we want to admit it or not, most closely resemble that older brother.

Which leads to my second question to all older sons and daughters: *Is it possible to get lost at home?*

I'm going to ask for a show of hands. Please raise your hand if you are a firstborn child. How many of you are firstborn? For those firstborn children, how many of you thought, "My younger brother, my younger sister — they get away with murder!"?

Another show of hands: How many of you here tonight are the youngest son or daughter in your family? Now, for those who raised your hands, how many of you younger children thought, "I never get to do anything!"?

Several studies indicate that parents do grow more lenient, the more children they have. They're more protective with the first, more demanding of the first.

I've personally observed parents in church. With their first child, if that first child picks up something and puts it in his mouth, it is a national health care crisis. With a second child, they let the child eat dirt and call it fiber. Some wise person remarked that with the third or fourth child, "You let them juggle knives!" Parents loosen up.

Perhaps because of these parenting differences, some psychologists tell us, firstborn children, like the older brother in our story, do stay home. They do want to please their parents. And they often, not always, but often, do what is expected.

The other side of all those positive traits is that sometimes, not always, but sometimes, firstborn children, or older siblings, or you or I, have the temptation to think, "I'm not getting what I deserve." The temptation is to grumble, to take things for granted, and to become cold to the riches you do have.

And when those temptations come close to our hearts, it's so easy to become lost at home. Some of us are prodigals who never went far away.

Notice in this story, the father says to the older son, "You have always been here and everything I have is yours." But did the older son appreciate the daily gift of his father's presence? Did the older

12

son feel profound gratitude for the riches that surrounded him? No.

That's the problem: he never enjoyed any of his father's blessings. He took things for granted. He became a stranger in his Father's house, striding around and thinking, "Poor me."

Are any of us like that? Do you enjoy forgiveness? Do you enjoy worship? Do you enjoy the peace that comes from following the Savior? Do you enjoy the capacity to give freely? Are we grateful?

Someone asked a terrible question: What if, when the prodigal son returned home, his father had not been there to meet him and instead he was met first by his older brother?

Now that would have been quite a plot change. With the older brother's lack of generosity, lack of compassion, and self-righteousness, he would sooner have killed his younger brother than embrace him.

Which leads to my third question: *Is it really possible to return home?* Or, to put it another way: Is it possible really to change?

The prodigal son changes. "He came to his senses" is the way scripture puts it. We don't know if the older brother changes. We know the father invites him to come in, to celebrate the prodigal's return, but we don't know if the older son said, "Yes," to his Father's invitation or whether he stood outside the party, clutching to his own cold self-righteousness. Is it possible really to change, to return home, whether you're lost in a far country or lost at home?

Of course, my answer to that question is yes. Change, real change, is possible.

During the season of Lent, traditionally Christians have worked hard at certain changes in our own personal lives. But *real change almost always requires a death*. Change requires a death.

"Coming to our senses" as the prodigal did, or returning, repenting, or perhaps like the elder son, swallowing our pride and joining the party — that requires a death which is terribly painful.

The Good News during Lent is that a death has occurred. God's own Son, giving his life for those lost in a far country, or those lost at home. God's own Son, showing us the depth, the greatness of God's love for each and every person, whether it is firstborn, middle child, or the baby of the family. God's own Son, Jesus Christ, spreading his arms wide on a cross, saying, "This love, this forgiveness, this power is for you, to change."

As we start our journey with Jesus to the cross, I have asked you three questions: To whom do you relate in the story of the Prodigal Son? Is it possible to get lost at home? Is it really possible to return home?

The Good News is that God holds you in the palm of his hand and loves you to death, whether you're in a far land, or lost at home. God offers you forgiveness, offers you a second chance, and offers you the power through Christ always to return home. Amen.

The Prodigal Son: "Sunrise Or Sunset?"

Luke 15:11ff: *And Jesus said, "There was a man who had two sons; and the younger of them said to his father, 'Father, give me the share of property that falls to me.' And he divided his living between them. Not many days later the younger son gathered all he had and took his journey into a far country, and there he squandered his property in loose living. And when he had spent everything, a great famine arose in that country, and he began to be in want. So he went and joined himself to one of the citizens of that country who sent him into his fields to feed swine...."*

(Setting: man dressed in Middle Eastern attire. His clothes are filthy and tattered, and he is shoeless. He leans over a shovel, seemingly exhausted from working. He squints towards the sky.)

Is that the sunrise or the sunset? I'm so tired, I'm not sure. I've been working so long in this pigsty. Talk about dead end jobs. My nostrils are filled with this filth.

Oh, you know me. My name's unimportant. You know my story though. Sometimes you call me the prodigal son. Hah! I've been called a lot worse, especially lately.

Is that the sunrise or the sunset?

You ask, "Why did you leave your home? How did you waste your money, your time, your life?"

I have some ready-made excuses for it all. I could speak of the need to look for something, something more. I searched in exotic places, fallen strangers, and forbidden desires for that something more. But in the end, it's all the same; it comes down to bad choices. Bad choices.

At the time, I was so young, I felt claustrophobic; I just had to get out. Home meant too many rules, too many obligations, and too much family. I just needed space.

Well, I sure found it. Now, I'm still young, but I feel old, tired. Is that the sunrise or the sunset?

As you know, I did the unthinkable. I asked my father for my inheritance. I assumed the old man would just turn me down flat, or worse, flatten me, disown me. But strange, strange, he gave me the money. Amazing.

You see, when I lived, asking for your inheritance was a mortal sin. A mortal sin against your parents and family.

You have a similar saying today when you say, "I wish you would drop dead!" When I asked for my inheritance, I was telling my father, "I wish you were dead!"

But he gave me the money. I still can't believe it. Amazing.

At first, I thought it was a dream come true. The answer to my prayers. I soon found out my so-called freedom was actually the beginning of my slavery.

How did I lose it all? What happened to the money? It's the old story of a fool. What's that saying, "A fool and his money are easily parted." I was that fool.

I wasted my inheritance — well, at least I'm good at something. It was a lot of money. But bad choices, bad choices. Well, at least in that way I was free. I was free to make terrible choices.

Your scripture says I went to a "far country." That's just another way of saying I rejected everything my family stood for. Not only did I leave, telling my father to drop dead, but I also left my family, my country, my home, my background, my friends, my religion ... my faith? I don't know.

Is that the sunrise or the sunset? I'm not sure anymore. One thing I do know, my so-called dream of doing things my way — how I wanted to live, with my stuff, with my future, with my life — has become my nightmare.

I wonder how my old man's doing? It's incredible, but back at the family farm the hired hands are treated better than this.

I wonder if it's changed? Home? I wonder if my older brother is still angry?

Is that the sunrise or the sunset? Hmm. I wonder — if I went home, would my old man give me even a job? Now as I think back on the life with my people, my family, my faith, at least there was food. There was work. I can still remember my father's last look. He looked me straight in the eyes and said, "I love you." Even after I wished him dead. "I love you." Amazing! I've got to get out of here. At least, at least to see my father's eyes one more time. See if that look is still there. If that look is still in his eyes, I'll know there's hope, hope for a second chance. Will he take me back? Will my father take me back? Will God take me back after all I've done? Is God Almighty the God of second chances? We will see. Is that the sunrise or the sunset? I hope it's the sunrise. Shalom.

Luke 15:17ff: *"But when he came to himself he said, 'How many of my father's hired servants have bread enough and to spare, but I perish here with hunger! I will arise and go to my father, and will say to him, "Father, I have sinned against heaven and before you; I am no longer worthy to be called your son; treat me as one of your hired servants." 'And he arose and came to his father. But while he was yet at a distance, his father saw him and had compassion, and ran and embraced him and kissed him...."*

17

The Elder Son: "The Coat Says It All"

Luke 15:25ff: *"Now his elder son was in the field; and as he came and drew near to the house, he heard music and dancing. And he called one of the servants and asked what this meant. And he said to him, 'Your brother has come and your father has killed the fatted calf, because he has received him safe and sound.' But the elder son was angry and refused to go in. His father came out and entreated him, but he answered his father, 'Lo, these many years I have served you, and I never disobeyed your command; yet you never gave me a kid, that I might make merry with my friends. But when this son of yours came, who has devoured your living with harlots, you killed for him the fatted calf!'"*

(Setting: man dressed in farming clothing, well-dressed, clean, wearing a jacket/vest/robe that is nice on the outside and perhaps torn or knotty on the inside.)

Shalom. My name is Achi [pronounced: Ah-key].

I know what you're going to say, why are you so mad? After all, your younger brother has returned, there's a party going on.

Before you get on my case, let me say a word of self-defense. I've always come off looking bad in this story. You say I'm jealous, self-righteous, judgmental, but we have a lot in common.

There are many older brothers and older sisters in this group tonight. You have the same good qualities as I have.

I love my family. I'm reliable. I'm dependable. I'm practical. I'm faithful. I work hard. I have lived my life according to God's law.

Let me ask you this: Who would you rather have as your banker? My younger brother, or me? As your doctor? As your son-in-law?

18

Who would you rather have watch your children, my wild younger brother or me? You wouldn't even let him in your house half the time.

Who would do better at farming? Who would make a better Sunday school teacher? Who would make a better husband? Who would make a better pastor?

The fact is, I've always gotten a bad rap. Your world wouldn't run if it wasn't for me. It's the elder brothers and older sisters of this world who build the hospitals and the shelters for the homeless, who feed the poor, who volunteer at church.

Give me a break. We have a lot in common.

So why did Rabbi Yeshua tell my story? Why did Rabbi Yeshua point out that not only was my younger brother lost in a distant country, but that I was lost at home? Why did Rabbi Yeshua tell my story?

Instead of telling you the reasons, let me show you the reasons.

Do you like my coat/vest/robe? Nice fabric. I paid 25 denarii for it. That's about a month's salary to you.

Nice coat on the outside. On the outside, I'm together, successful, industrious, prosperous. But on the inside of this coat, it's all knotted up.

By telling my story, I believe Rabbi Yeshua reminds us to look beyond the level of appearances.

On the outside, all of us can put on our stage face, but on the inside, every single person — me, you — we all have issues to deal with. Not one person is without sin.

The second reason Rabbi Yeshua told my story is that we all want to be self-sufficient, and that's a good thing. But at the same time we need to realize that all of life is a gift.

My father reminded me of this when I wouldn't join the party. My father came out to me and said, "Son, you are always with me. And all that I have is yours."

My father reminded me that we take so much for granted, even life itself. Even God's grace.

The final thing I believe Rabbi Yeshua was reminding us through this story: God gives us opportunities to change.

19

Rabbi Yeshua finished his story by saying that I stood outside. Did I join the party? Did I realize that I too have been blessed by God? Did I decide to change from ingratitude to laughter at the mere joy of living? Did I join God's party?

One thing you may not realize: like my younger brother, I publicly disgraced my father too. My public disgrace was demanding that my father come out to me. No obedient Jewish son would ever disgrace his father in such a way.

That kind of disobedience could get you killed in my time. And not to join a party that my father had organized, that too is a public humiliation for my father.

And yet my father still came out to me. He's not your traditional parent. He still came out to me. That's my father. That's our God.

Did I go in? Did I join the party after my father went so far to include me? Did I join God's party? Especially after God went so far to remind me that everything I have is a gift.

Well, Rabbi Yeshua doesn't say. That's up to you to decide.

I'll let you in on a secret. I told you my name is Achi. In Hebrew that means "my brother." Achi — my brother. You see, it's really not my story; I'm your brother. This is your story.

Rabbi Yeshua is asking you to change. Change from judging people by external appearances. Change from thinking that life somehow owes you something, and instead see life as a gift. Change from prideful isolation to joyfully entering God's party of life.

Did I go in? Will you go in? My brother, my sister?

Shalom.

Luke 15:31-32: *"And the father said to his elder son, 'Son, you are always with me, and all that is mine is yours. It was fitting to make merry and be glad, for this your brother was dead, and is alive; he was lost, and is found.'"*

The Father: "Not Your Typical Parent"

Luke 15:20-24: *"And the prodigal son arose and returned to his father. But while he was yet at a distance, his father saw him and had compassion, and ran and embraced him and kissed him. And the son said to him, 'Father, I have sinned against heaven and before you; I am no longer worthy to be called your son.' But the father said to his servants, 'Bring quickly the best robe, and put it on him; and put a ring on his hand, and shoes on his feet; and bring the fatted calf and kill it, and let us eat and make merry; for this my son was dead, and is alive again; he was lost, and is found.' "*

(Setting: man dressed in first century, Middle Eastern attire. He holds a large clay pot or jar.)

Have you ever done something that's so outrageous, so bizarre, so extravagant, it gets your neighbors talking, gets your neighborhood talking, gets your whole town talking?

Well, let me tell you about a time I was on the receiving end of a ton of gossip.

My two sons. You know them well. But let me tell you some things about the story and about our family you've probably never heard before.

I'm not your typical parent, at least not in my time.

First, when my youngest son asked for his inheritance, according to tradition I would have beaten him senseless and then driven him out of the house penniless. Instead I gave him his inheritance. I'm not your typical parent.

Second, I was always on the lookout for my prodigal son. You see, I know my children. They are very different in strengths and weaknesses. I love each of them totally, but they are different.

I knew my younger son would fail, probably lose all his inheritance. To be officially welcomed back to our village he would have to endure the *qetsatsah* ceremony.[3] What's the *qetsatsah* ceremony?

The Talmud, our sacred writing, has prescribed a certain punishment for any child who lost the family inheritance to Gentiles: the *qetsatsah* ceremony.

The ceremony is simple. The villagers would bring a large earthenware jar, pottery, fill it with burned nuts and burned corn, and break it in front of the guilty individual. While doing this, the community would shout, "The person is cut off from his people." From that point on, the village would have nothing to do with my son.

In your day, you have the term of "shun" or "excommunicate." But it's much more than this. Our Jewish shunning is a total ban on any contact with the violator.

So you see, I had a plan. I wanted to reach my son before he got to our village. If I reached out to my son, if I publicly humbled myself and was able to reconcile publicly with my son, no one would dare suggest that the ceremony be enacted. I'm not your typical parent.

Third, in my day, mothers could run down the road and shower the boy with kisses. Mothers could show public affection. That's fine. But not the father. I'm expected to sit in grand isolation in the house to hear what the boy might have to say for himself.

But I couldn't contain myself. To both my older and my younger sons, I was hands-on, running out to meet them, showing them affection. I'm a father who acts like a mother. I'm not your typical parent.

Honestly, I am only human. I am a father who loves and hates, forgives and holds grudges, wise and also painfully ignorant. But the Rabbi Yeshua told this story to explain Yahweh's ways.

First, it's about *hesed* — love. Not just any mushy, soft, feel-good love, but hard, strong, unlimited love. *Hesed.* Yahweh is love.

Second, it's about freedom.

Yahweh has given each person an incredible, wonderful, and, at times, very painful gift — freedom. We are free to turn away. We are free to run and run and run until we die. And we are always free to return home.

In my story, I give my wayward son shoes, a robe, and a ring. There's an important lesson about Yahweh here.

In my day, bare feet indicated slavery; shoes meant safety, strength. Yahweh doesn't want us to think of ourselves as inferior people, but as children of God. Not as second class citizens, not as hired hands or servants, but holy, chosen, and beloved.

But we are still free to take off the shoes, take off the robe, and remove the ring.

Third, it's about intimacy.

In my story, I throw a party, not just any party but an end-all bash. I throw it for my younger son and I plead with my older son to forget the law for a minute and think of relationships. Forget the revenge for a minute and think about the future. Forget the past for a minute and remember the blessings that surround him. I throw a party for both children.

Yahweh invites us to a party, a meal, and an invitation to intimacy. That's the invitation to my children and that's God's invitation to you. An invitation to intimacy with God.

Well, that's my story. I'm not your typical parent. It's really not my story. It's God's story. He doesn't play by the rules either, at least not our rules. And he's always inviting you to return home. Shalom.

> Luke 15:28-32: *"But the older son was angry and refused to go in. His father came out and begged him, but he answered his father, 'Lo, these many years I have served you, and I never disobeyed your command; yet you never gave me a kid, that I might make merry with my friends. But when this son of yours came, who has devoured your living with harlots, you killed for him the fatted calf!' And he said to him, 'Son, you are always with me, and all that is mine is yours. It was fitting to make merry and be glad, for this your brother was dead, and is alive; he was lost, and is found.'"*

The Mother: "Where's Mom?"

Luke 15:22-23: *"The Father said to his servants, 'Quick! Bring out the best robe and put it on him; put a ring on his finger and sandals on his feet. Bring the calf we have been fattening, and kill it; we will celebrate by having a banquet, because this son of mine was dead and has come back to life....'"*

(Setting: woman dressed in Middle Eastern attire, perhaps in black, suggesting mourning. Or, if the sanctuary permits this form of application, have the woman stand in the back out of sight and speak through a microphone.)

"Where's Mom?" Have you ever wondered, "Where's Mom?"

In Yeshua's story of the Prodigal Son, have you ever wondered, "Where's Mom?" Why did Jesus leave me out of this story?

I'm sure there are many today who would say, "Well, Jesus is just telling a story in a way acceptable to that time and place."

In that time and place, women were not spoken of, were not thought of, were not taught. They had their place and their place was to be silent.

That includes all women, not just mothers. A prayer from a Jewish boy of my time went, "Thank You, God Almighty, that I was not born a gentile or a woman."

Where's the mother of the prodigal? A simple answer: I was not important enough to be included by Yeshua.

But, maybe that's too simple. I'm talking about the Rabbi Yeshua, and there's nothing simple about him.

At every turn, Jesus was doing the unexpected. At every turn, Jesus was stepping across man-made boundaries of race and gender.

That's certainly one of the things that got him killed. Yeshua looked beyond stereotypes, beyond labels, beyond race, beyond our past, deep into the heart to see God's image.

Of course, just before Yeshua told the story of the Prodigal Son he told another story about a woman searching for a lost coin.

You see, the simple truth is that Yeshua told stories of women, he talked to women, he traveled with them, taught them, even touched them.

Is it a coincidence that a woman, Mary Magdalene, was the first to see Jesus risen from the dead? Is it simple coincidence that it was a woman who was the first evangelist, the first teller of good news? It's not that simple.

Where's the mother in the story of the Prodigal Son? A simplistic answer would be, Jesus told a story that was acceptable for the time. But that would not be the truth.

Where am I in this story? Where's the prodigal's mother? The answer is so clear it's easy to miss. The answer is so self-evident, it's easy to overlook. The answer is at the same time a very tragic one.

Where was I? I was dead. I died giving birth to my youngest son. I died giving birth to the prodigal.

When I lived, nearly 2000 years ago, nearly half of all children died within the first year of birth. And mothers giving birth, an extremely high number of us died in labor.

Where's the mother of the prodigal? I was dead. I died giving life to the prodigal.

Since that time, I've been in what some call the balcony of faith. I am part of what your Creed calls "the communion of saints."

So what have I learned about this Yeshua? What have I learned from Yahweh in the balcony of faith, this communion of saints?

First, because of God's extravagant, prodigal love, even death is not the end.

In Yeshua's story, at the return of the prodigal, my husband throws a banquet. A banquet. A great feast.

The reason Yeshua speaks of a banquet is because a banquet is a symbol for life. Where God is, there is life. Where God is, there is joy. And not even death can sing finally at God's banquet.

My husband said it well when the prodigal returned, "... we will celebrate by having a banquet, because this son of mine was dead and has come back to life...."

As the mother of the prodigal son, I have learned that because of Yahweh's love; even death is not the end.

The second thing I've learned as the mother of the prodigal son: don't give up on people.

Yeshua looked beyond appearances, beyond their past, beyond the surface to see each person as created in the image of God. He never gave up on people.

If this story means anything, it means God has a big family. God includes, when we want to exclude. God invites, when we stand at a distance. God runs to meet, when we look the other way. God has a big family because He never gives up on people.

I mentioned Rabbi Yeshua spoke of a banquet and how a banquet is symbolic of heaven. A banquet is also symbolic and foreshadows Holy Communion.

Each week, around the world, people hear of Yeshua giving his body, shedding his blood out of love.

That banquet table is the largest table in the world because of God's grace. It has to be the largest table in the world because God has a large family. Don't give up on people.

Finally, as the mother of the prodigal son, I've learned that I'm not always in control.

I died giving birth to my son. I was not in control then. I was not in control when my youngest son wanted to waste his life. I was not in control when my oldest son slowly turned cold to everyone, even life.

Realizing that I couldn't control my adult sons didn't mean I stopped praying for them. Realizing that I couldn't put things right for them didn't mean I stopped crying for them.

Where was the mother? I was right here all along. Making a painful journey myself, realizing that I am not only a mother, at times tormented by my children, but also learning to be a trusting daughter — waiting on Yahweh.

Where was the mother? I was making that long journey — realizing that I am not always in charge, in control. I am slowly learning to be a trusting daughter — trusting our Heavenly Father. Perhaps, perhaps, that's the longest journey home.

Shalom.

Luke 15:32: *"But it was only right we should celebrate and rejoice, because your brother here was dead and has come to life; he was lost and is found."*

The Servant: "Can I Get A Witness?"

Luke 15:22ff: *"But the father said to his servants,
'Quick! Bring the best robe and put it on him. Put
a ring on his finger and sandals on his feet. Bring
the fattened calf and kill it. Let's have a feast and
celebrate....'"*

(Setting: person dressed in Middle Eastern attire, perhaps with a
notepad, reporting, like a news reporter.)

Observing. Watching. Examining from the outside, from a distance. That's what I have been doing. I am the servant. Tonight, I
am a witness.

In Jesus' story of the prodigal son, you have heard from all the
main people. You have heard from the prodigal son, his side of the
story. You have heard from the elder son, his side of the story. You
have heard from the father, his side of the story. You have even
heard from the mother, her side of the story.

Like pieces of a jigsaw puzzle, you have heard from each family member. You notice how each person looked at things differ-
ently. You notice how each describes this story of Rabbi Yeshua
from a different angle.

Tonight, in closing, I would like to tell you my observations. I
am the servant. I watched from a distance as the father and his
prodigal son embraced, awkwardly. I was the servant the father
called to begin the arrangements for the large party.

I am the servant the older son met as he heard the party going
on. I observed the anger, the feeling of betrayal etched across his
face. I watched from a distance as the father came out to the older
son. I watched the father plead with his older son and I watched the
hatred grow in the son's eyes.

I am the servant, the witness. Tonight, I will put the many pieces
of the story together and add a few of my own. Together, in place,

all the pieces of the puzzle tell the same story — God's unrelenting love in the face of our pettiness.

First, let me set the record straight about the prodigal son's crime. What was his crime?

He is often accused of immorality, sexual sin. As a matter of fact, his older brother evens yells it out, "This boy has squandered your property with prostitutes!"

But what are the facts? Rabbi Yeshua says nothing about prostitutes. That's what the jealous older brother wants you to believe.

Rabbi Yeshua instead says, "Loose living." The Hebrew word does not imply prostitutes; it does not even imply sexual immorality, but being a spendthrift.

The older brother clearly wants to exaggerate his brother's failures.

Don't we all do that? Exaggerate our brother's, our sister's failures, all the while putting the best possible light on our words and actions. What do you call it today, "spin doctoring."

Your own church leader, Martin Luther, said the following about bearing false witness. He said, "We are to fear and love God so that we do not betray, slander, or lie about our neighbor, but defend him, speak well of him, and explain his actions in the kindest way."

Let me set the record straight. The prodigal son was guilty of many things, but let's not act morally superior and pile on more crimes that are not in Rabbi Yeshua's story.

Second, let me set the record straight about the prodigal son's so-called confession.

The prepared confession reads, "I have sinned against heaven and before you." This is usually seen as heartfelt repentance.

But Rabbi Yeshua is so wise. He has the prodigal quoting scripture in that place. And what scripture is the prodigal son quoting, you ask?

The confession is a quote from the Pharaoh of Egypt. The pharaoh makes this same confession when he tried to manipulate Moses into lifting the plagues!

After the ninth plague, Pharaoh finally agrees to meet Moses, and when Moses appears, Pharaoh gives the same speech, "I have sinned against heaven and before you." But everyone knows that

Pharaoh is not repenting. He is simply trying to bend Moses to his will.

The prodigal, at best, is attempting the same. Hoping to cleverly soften his father's heart.

So, let me set the record straight about the prodigal's so-called confession. It was not at the heart of this story. It was not what won the father over. It was not what changed the father's heart.

Above all, it was the father's love that even accepted a sinful, weak, desperate confession. That's the heart of this story. Is that good news for you?

Finally, let me set the record straight about the family. This is more than a family story. This is a community story.

With your homes, your neighborhoods, your televisions, your electronic garage door openers, you can come and go, live your own little lives, within your own little family, but that's not the way it is in my time.

What affected one person, affected us all. What the prodigal did to the father, he did to the whole community. What the older brother did in not coming into the party was a public disgrace against his father, a public sin against our community.

This is not a family story. This is a community story.

What is your family story? What is your community story?

Is this a family of judgment? Or is this a community of grace and reconciliation?

Is this a family that asks people to prove their worthiness before accepting them back? Or is this a community that welcomes all sinners?

Is this a family that does not hear the cries of people living without God? Or is this a community that constantly looks beyond itself to the needs of the neighbor?

Is this a family that is preoccupied with its own rights, its own needs, its own kind? Or is this a community that is generous, takes risks, laughs at its failures and tries again?

I am the servant, a witness. Let me set the record straight. This is not a family story. This is a community story.

Tonight, I have laid out the rest of Rabbi Yeshua's puzzle. You have heard from the prodigal. You have heard from the elder brother.

You have heard from the father. You have even heard from the prodigal's own mother. All the pieces of the puzzle are now before you.

And now that we have put all the pieces together, what do we see? A painting, a masterpiece of God's unrelenting love for all people. A masterpiece of God's unrelenting love painted in blood from a cross. We see a painting, a masterpiece of God's unrelenting love that will not give up, until all people return home.

Shalom.

> Luke 15:25ff: *"Meanwhile, the older son was in the field. When he came near the house, he heard music and dancing. So he called one of the servants and asked him what was going on. 'Your brother has come,' he replied, 'and your father has killed the fattened calf because he has him back safe and sound.' The older brother became angry and refused to go in. So his father went out and pleaded with him. But he answered his father, 'Look! All these years I've been slaving for you and never disobeyed your orders. Yet you never gave me even a young goat so I could celebrate with my friends. But when this son of yours who has squandered your property with prostitutes comes home, you kill the fattened calf for him!' 'My son,' the father said, 'you are always with me, and everything I have is yours. But we had to celebrate and be glad, because this brother of yours was dead and is alive again; he was lost and is found.'"*

Closing The Distance

Luke 15:20b: *"But while the prodigal son was still at a distance, his father saw him and was filled with compassion for him; he ran to his son, threw his arms around him and kissed him...."*

Matthew 27:55-56: *Many women were also there, looking on from a distance; they had followed Jesus from Galilee and had provided for him. Among them were Mary Magdalene, and Mary the mother of James and Joseph, and the mother of the sons of Zebedee.*

When my daughter Emma was two years old, she was observing me getting robed up for Sunday worship. She watched with great interest as first I put on the outer, white alb. Then, I tied a white rope, the belt, around my waist. Next, I put a heavy cross around my neck. Finally, I put on a purple stole.

As I ceremoniously put on these outer garments, Emma's eyes grew wider and wider with amazement until finally she asked very deliberately, "Daddy, are you a king?"

I responded, "Well, as a matter of fact...." I wish I could have recorded her question for those times she views me as less than royal.

Tonight, Jesus is crowned as royalty, not with a clean white robe, but with a crown of thorns, with a purple robe stained with blood, and a vicious cross his throne.

This nightmare of an enthronement he endures because whether we accept it or not, whether we doubt it or not, whether we want to believe it or not — for him, he endured this enthronement out of love, for us. And so tonight, Jesus extends his arms to the ends of the universe and says, "This is how much I love you!"

It is that love from the cross that has flowed down through the centuries like a stream in a desert. It is a love that has flown to all classes, cultures, races, and countries. For 2,000 years that stream of love has meandered through human hearts bringing life to people dying of thirst.

In Saint Matthew's Gospel, a portion of that bloody enthronement is reported. Jesus was crucified and women stood by *"looking on from a distance."*

I'm indebted to Pastor Will Willimon for pointing out that the Greek word for distance is *makron*.[4]

The women weren't too close, but at a distance, a *makron*. After all, a man was being murdered. Any sane person would stand "at a distance."

Later that night, that word *makron* is used again. When Jesus is led away in the darkness to be interrogated, tortured, and condemned, Saint Matthew reports that Peter followed "at a distance." While Jesus was beaten in the chamber above, Peter cowered around a fire, denying his Lord, three times and standing "at a distance."

Now you see, *makron* is more than a physical, geographical description, but is a spiritual word. The women, Peter, the other disciples were "at a distance" spiritually. So many times, in terms of faith, we also follow, but "at a distance."

As we look at Jesus' passion and compassion, Jesus' love and courage, Jesus' faith and hope compared to ours, we stand "at a distance."

When we hear God's call to care for the hungry, the sick, the homeless, the grieving, and observe what we actually do, then we know, deep down, we stand "at a distance" from God.

When we look at the commitment of the saints, when we read of the enthusiasm with which they gave their lives to Jesus, and when we note our following on stumbling feet, we know we stand "at a distance" from whom God calls us to be.

Makron. Distance. There is another place this little word is found and that is the story of the Prodigal Son. We have been looking at this story throughout the season of Lent and now we see the word *makron* also there. In Luke's story of the prodigal son, Jesus says that the father was waiting for his lost son to return home. When he sees him (*makron*) at a distance, the father comes running and embraces the prodigal. He does not wait for the prodigal son's repentance or recommitment, but he runs, bridges the distance, and embraces.

Where are you tonight? Are you feeling close to God or are you at a distance?

The good news is that God doesn't wait for us to get our acts together, clean up our lives, or make a commitment to him before he comes running to us. Jesus stretches his arms out on a cross. He comes to us and closes the distance. He reaches out across the great distance of our sin, our guilt, our shame, our fear, determined to bring us home, to bring us close.

Tonight, we are standing like those women of long ago, standing before the cross, but at a distance. Tonight, Jesus dies, giving his love to us and to all that are "at a distance."

I'm not sure where this story originates but it speaks of God's closing the distance:

Two newlyweds were on their honeymoon, on the "loveboat." The first night they went to eat at the table to which they had been assigned. They discovered that they were seated with a young woman and an older man. Much to their discomfort, the older man's face was terribly disfigured.

Because of the horrible disfigurement, the people at the table lost their appetites. The newlywed couple politely excused themselves early. They could not eat and simultaneously look at his wretched face.

After the previous night's experience, the young couple decided not to show up for breakfast the next morning. And again, they politely declined their lunch invitation as well. They simply could not stand the thought of trying to eat in the presence of that face. They felt they could not look up and they certainly could not make conversation.

That afternoon, as the couple was lounging around the pool, the young woman who had been sitting with the older man found the couple and spoke to them the following words:

"I noticed how upset you were last night and that you didn't come to either breakfast or lunch today. I think I know what the problem is — it's the man with the disfigured face, right? He's my father. Let me tell you what happened to him.

"Years ago, when I was still a child, our house caught on fire during the night. My father led my mother and me out of the burning wreck. Through the smoke, fire, and collapsing structures, we became separated. My father could have easily escaped, but once he realized that we were not with him, that we were still trapped inside, back inside he ran.

"My father ran back inside, again and again. At one point, nearly exhausted, weeping, he broke past the fireman's barricade and rushing into the house, found me and carried me to safety. Then he went back in again and again to find my mother. But he was too late to save her.

"The price of his loving search is his terribly disfigured face. So you see, to me, it's the most beautiful face in the world. I just thought you'd like to know."

Tonight, on the cross, we see the price of God's loving search. The cost was a terribly painful enthronement. What does this night mean to you? Well, that's up to you. I hope it totally captures, captivates, enlivens your life, and closes the distance. Tonight, Jesus spreads his arms and says, "This is how much I love you, and all people."

This love is available to all, even those, especially those, who are "at a distance." Amen.

Order Of Worship
Ash Wednesday

Welcome! Our theme for Lent is "Returning Home." You do have an eternal home because of the life, death, and resurrection of Jesus. On this night, we recall that we are but dust, and yet, not even the grave can destroy the love of God. May you experience God's forgiveness!

The Prelude

The Hymn   "I Want Jesus To Walk With Me"
                                                          (#660 WOV)

The Invocation and Opening Prayer

The Old Testament Reading (*Read responsively*)   Joel 2:12-14
    L: Yet even now, says the Lord, return to me with all your heart, with fasting, with weeping, and with mourning. Rend your hearts and not your clothing.

    C: Return to the Lord, your God, for he is gracious and merciful, slow to anger, and abounding in steadfast love.

    L: Who knows whether he will not turn and relent, and leave a blessing behind him, a grain offering and a drink offering for the Lord, your God?

    C: Return to the Lord, your God, for he is gracious and merciful, slow to anger, and abounding in steadfast love.

    L: Why should it be said among the peoples, "Where is their God?"

    C: Return to the Lord, your God, for he is gracious and merciful, slow to anger, and abounding in steadfast love.

Special Music

The Psalm (*Read responsively*)   Psalm 51:1-5, 9-13
Have mercy on me, O God, according to your loving-kindness;
in your great compassion blot out my offenses.

Wash me through and through from my wickedness,
and cleanse me from my sin.

For I know my transgressions,
and my sin is ever before me.

Against you only have I sinned
and done what is evil in your sight.

And so you are justified when you speak
and upright in your judgment.

Make me hear of joy and gladness
that the body you have broken may rejoice.

Hide your face from my sins,
and blot out all my iniquities.

Create in me a clean heart, O God,
and renew a right spirit within me.

Cast me not away from your presence,
and take not your Holy Spirit from me.

Give me the joy of your saving help again,
and sustain me with your bountiful Spirit.

The Epistle Reading   2 Corinthians 5:20b—6:10

The Holy Gospel   Luke 15:11-32

Special Music

The Theme Hymn "Our Father, We Have Wandered"
(#733 WOV)

The Message Getting Lost At Home

The Offering

The Offertory Music

The Offertory Prayer
As you have been bountiful to us, O God, we would be generous in supporting the programs and mission of your church. Help us to find the right priorities for all you entrust to us, that our hearts may follow our treasure to their rightful home; through Jesus Christ, your Son, our Lord. Amen.

The Prayers
(*After each prayer:* Lord, in your mercy, **hear our prayer**.)

The Lord's Prayer

The Blessing Of Ashes
God our Creator, you sent your beloved Son, Jesus, to be our brother. The burden of your love for humankind led him to accept death, death on a cross, so that all people might live. Though we were buried with Christ in baptism and raised up to a new life of freedom, we have not lived fully as your sons and daughters; your reign of love and justice is still not fully manifest in us. Bless these ashes and your people whose heads shall be marked with ashes. Grant that this may be a symbol of our inner renewal, a sign of our change and growth, a first step in our returning home to your love; through Jesus Christ, your Son, our Lord. Amen.

The Imposition Of Ashes

The Hymn During Imposition   "Create In Me A Clean Heart"
(#732 WOV)

The Words Of Forgiveness

The Blessing

The Recessional Hymn   "Joyful, Joyful We Adore Thee"
(#551 LBW)

The Closing Words
Leader: Go in peace. Serve the Lord.
People: Thanks be to God!

The Postlude

Order Of Worship
Wednesday Lent 1

*Welcome to worship this evening. Tonight, we will hear from Jesus'
story of the Prodigal Son. May the music, the message, and this
time of prayer remind you of the Son's great love for you, a compassion that sent him to a cross.*

Returning Home

(The slide of Rembrandt's painting, *The Return Of The Prodigal
Son*, will be shown. As you focus on the kneeling prodigal, may
this time deepen your personal meditation on returning home to
Christ.)

The Prelude

The Welcome and Announcements

The Hymn "Bind Us Together"
(#748 WOV)

The Prayer Of The Day
Lord God, we thank you for a home to return to, when we feel
all alone. We thank you for a home to long for, when we feel
lost. We thank you for a home to work towards, when we feel
a lack of purpose. Remind us tonight and each day that you
indeed are our home. Remind us tonight and each day that our
hearts are restless, until they rest completely in you; through
your Son, Jesus Christ our Lord. Amen.

The Old Testament Reading Hosea 14:1-7

The New Testament Reading Ephesians 2:1-8

The Hymn "There's A Wideness In God's Mercy"
(#290 LBW)

The Message   The Prodigal Son: "Sunrise Or Sunset?"

The Theme Hymn   "Our Father, We Have Wandered"
               (#733 WOV)

The Offering

The Offertory Music

The Offertory Prayer
 Merciful Father, you are always willing to welcome home those
who have wandered from your grace. For this hope and so much
more we are eternally thankful. May this offering truly be an
outward expression of our gratitude and may it be used to further your reign on earth; through your Son, Jesus Christ our
Lord. Amen.

The Prayers
 (*After each prayer:* Lord, in your mercy, **hear our prayer**.)

The Lord's Prayer

The Blessing

The Hymn   "Let Us Talents And Tongues Employ"
               (#754 WOV)

The Closing Words
 Leader: Go in peace. Serve the Lord.
 People: Thanks be to God!

The Postlude

Order Of Worship
Wednesday Lent 2

Welcome to worship this evening. Tonight, we will hear again from Jesus' story of the Prodigal Son. May the music, the message, and this time of prayer remind you of the Son's great love for you, a compassion that sent him to a cross.

Returning Home

(The slide of Rembrandt's painting, *The Return Of The Prodigal Son,* focuses on the portion showing the older brother. May this visual deepen your personal meditation on returning home to Christ.)

The Prelude

The Welcome and Announcements

The Hymn   "My Lord Of Light"
                                            (#796 WOV)

The Prayer Of The Day
> Lord God, we thank you for a home to return to, when we feel all alone. We thank you for a home to long for, when we feel lost. We thank you for a home to work towards, when we feel a lack of purpose. Remind us tonight and each day that you indeed are our home. Remind us tonight and each day that our hearts are restless, until they rest completely in you; through your Son, Jesus Christ our Lord. Amen.

The Old Testament Reading   Isaiah 61:10-11

The New Testament Reading   1 John 1:5-10

The Hymn   "Alas! And Did My Savior Bleed"
                                            (#98 LBW)

43

The Message	The Elder Son: "The Coat Says It All"

The Theme Hymn	"Our Father, We Have Wandered"
	(#733 WOV)

The Offering

The Offertory Music

The Offertory Prayer

Loving God, it is so easy to become lost, even while at home; to take for granted your many blessings, even while surrounded by your riches. Help us always to acknowledge your generosity in all that we say and do. May this offering be a symbol of our inward renewal as we offer ourselves to you; through our Lord and Savior, Jesus Christ. Amen.

The Prayers

(*After each prayer:* Lord, in your mercy, **hear our prayer.**)

The Lord's Prayer

The Blessing

The Hymn	"Wash, O God ..."
	(#697 WOV)

The Closing Words

Leader: Go in peace. Serve the Lord.
People: Thanks be to God!

The Postlude

Order Of Worshp
Wednesday Lent 3

Welcome to worship this evening. Tonight, we will hear again from Jesus' story of the Prodigal Son. May the music, the message, and this time of prayer remind you of the Son's great love for you, a compassion that sent him to a cross.

Returning Home

(The slide of Rembrandt's painting *The Return Of The Prodigal Son* focuses on the portion showing the father. May this visual deepen your personal meditation on returning home to Christ.)

The Prelude

The Welcome and Announcements

The Hymn "I Was There To Hear Your Borning Cry"
(#770 WOV)

The Prayer Of The Day
Lord God, we thank you for a home to return to, when we feel all alone. We thank you for a home to long for, when we feel lost. We thank you for a home to work towards, when we feel a lack of purpose. Remind us tonight and each day that you indeed are our home. Remind us tonight and each day that our hearts are restless, until they rest completely in you; through your Son, Jesus Christ our Lord. Amen.

The Old Testament Reading Hosea 11:1-4

The New Testament Reading Romans 8:12-17

The Hymn "Amazing Grace"
(#448 LBW)

The Message   The Father: "Not Your Typical Parent"

The Theme Hymn   "Our Father, We Have Wandered"
(#733 WOV)

The Offering

The Offertory Music

The Offertory Prayer
Your good and gracious will is done, even without our praying for it, Holy Father. But we ask now that it would be done through our lives. May our offering express our gratitude for all you have done in our lives and for the furthering of your will on earth; through your Son, Jesus Christ our Lord. Amen.

The Prayers
(*After each prayer:* Lord, in your mercy, **hear our prayer**.)

The Lord's Prayer

The Blessing

The Hymn   "Thy Holy Wings"
(#741 WOV)

The Closing Words
Leader: Go in peace. Serve the Lord.
People: Thanks be to God!

The Postlude

Order Of Worship
Wednesday Lent 4

Welcome to worship this evening. Tonight, we will hear again from Jesus' story of the Prodigal Son. May the music, the message, and this time of prayer remind you of the Son's great love for you, a compassion that sent him to a cross.

Returning Home

(The slide of Rembrandt's painting, *The Return Of The Prodigal Son*, will focus on the portion showing the hands of the father. Many commentaries on this painting point out the fact that the two hands are very different. The left hand is very masculine. It is the hand of a father. The right hand is very feminine. It is a woman's hand, perhaps even a mother's. As we hear from the mother of the prodigal, may her testimony and this visual deepen your personal meditation on returning home to Christ.)

The Prelude

The Welcome and Announcements

The Hymn   "O Christ the Same"
                                                        (#778 WOV)

The Prayer Of The Day
Lord God, we thank you for a home to return to, when we feel all alone. We thank you for a home to long for, when we feel lost. We thank you for a home to work towards, when we feel a lack of purpose. Remind us tonight and each day that you indeed are our home. Remind us tonight and each day that our hearts are restless, until they rest completely in you; through your Son, Jesus Christ our Lord. Amen.

The Old Testament Reading   Isaiah 49:5-6, 14-16

47

The New Testament Reading   1 Corinthians 15:51-58

The Hymn   "For All The Saints" (vv. 1, 4)
                                                  (#174 LBW)

The Message   The Mother: "Where's Mom?"

The Theme Hymn   "Our Father, We Have Wandered"
                                                  (#733 WOV)

The Offering

The Offertory Music

The Offertory Prayer
    Lord God, you have surrounded us with so great a cloud of
    witnesses — those saints, both known and unknown who pro-
    claimed your merciful reign. May our offerings be used to fur-
    ther their proclamation of your Son and so at the last, we may
    share eternally the joy you have set before them; through your
    Son, Jesus Christ our Lord. Amen.

The Prayers
    (*After each prayer:* Lord, in your mercy, **hear our prayer**.)

The Lord's Prayer

The Blessing

The Hymn   "For All Your Saints, O Lord"
                                                  (#176 LBW)

The Closing Words
    Leader: Go in peace. Serve the Lord.
    People: Thanks be to God!

The Postlude

48

Order Of Worship
Wednesday Lent 5

Welcome to worship this evening. Tonight, we will hear again from Jesus' story of the Prodigal Son. May the music, the message, and this time of prayer remind you of the Son's great love for you, a compassion that sent him to a cross.

Returning Home

The slide of Rembrandt's painting, *The Return Of The Prodigal Son*, focuses on the portion showing the servant. May this visual deepen your personal meditation on returning home to Christ.)

The Prelude

The Welcome and Announcements

The Hymn   "I, The Lord Of Sea And Sky"
                                                              (#752 WOV)

The Prayer Of The Day
  Lord God, we thank you for a home to return to, when we feel all alone. We thank you for a home to long for, when we feel lost. We thank you for a home to work towards, when we feel a lack of purpose. Remind us tonight and each day that you indeed are our home. Remind us tonight and each day that our hearts are restless, until they rest completely in you; through your Son, Jesus Christ our Lord. Amen.

The Old Testament Reading   Isaiah 43:1-13

The New Testament Reading   Romans 13:8-10

The Hymn   "What Wondrous Love Is This"
                                                              (#385 LBW)

The Message The Servant: "Can I Get A Witness?"

The Theme Hymn "Our Father, We Have Wandered"
(#733 WOV)

The Offering

The Offertory Music

The Offering Prayer
Loving God, it is your will for all people to return home to your grace. Use our offerings to further your loving call to all people. May these offerings be a symbol of our inner desire to be a part of that mission, a mission that led your Son to a cross; in his holy name we pray. Amen.

The Prayers
(*After each prayer:* (Lord, in your mercy, **hear our prayer**.)

The Lord's Prayer

The Blessing

The Hymn "Let Us Talents And Tongues Employ"
(#754 WOV)

The Closing Words
Leader: Go in peace. Serve the Lord.
People: Thanks be to God!

The Postlude

Order Of Worship
Good Friday Tenebrae

Welcome to worship on this Good Friday. Tonight is a tenebrae service. Tenebrae means darkening or shadows. During the service, the sanctuary will slowly grow darker as we hear the last words spoken by Jesus from the cross. This is a quiet and meditative service. We will ponder the awesome love of Christ on the cross and what this means for our daily living. May this time of reflection and renewal be a good preparation for your Easter celebration.

The Prelude
    (*A time for silent reflection*)

The Call To Worship   "Pie Jesu" (Merciful Jesus) by Andrew Lloyd Weber

The Song   "Were You There" (vv. 1-2)
    (*Please remain seated*)   (#92 LBW)

The First Word From The Cross   Luke 23:33-34

Solo Meditation   "Jesus, In Thy Dying Woes" (vv. 1-2)
         (#112 LBW)

Extinguishing Of The First Candle

Special Music

The Second Word From The Cross   Luke 23:39-43

Solo Meditation   "Jesus, In Thy Dying Woes" (vv. 4-5)

Extinguishing Of The Second Candle

The Offering

Special Music During The Offering

The Third Word From The Cross   John 19:26-27

Solo Meditation   "Jesus, In Thy Dying Woes" (vv. 7-8)

Extinguishing Of The Third Candle

The Song   "Ah, Holy Jesus"
(#123 LBW)

The Message   Closing The Distance

The Fourth Word From The Cross   Matthew 27:45

Solo Meditation   "Jesus, In Thy Dying Woes" (vv. 10-11)

Extinguishing Of The Fourth Candle

The Prayers
(*After each prayer:* Lord, in your mercy, **hear our prayer**.)

The Lord's Prayer

The Placing Of The Drops Of Wine On The Altar
(*The Pastor places five drops of wine on the altar, representing
the five wounds of Christ: the hands, the feet, and the side.*)

The Fifth Word From The Cross   John 19:28-29

Solo Meditation   "Jesus, In Thy Dying Woes" (vv. 13, 15)

Extinguishing Of The Fifth Candle

The Song   "O Sacred Head, Now Wounded" (vv. 1, 3)
(#117 LBW)

The Covering Of The Cross

The Sixth Word From The Cross   Luke 23:44-46

Solo Meditation   "Jesus, In Thy Dying Woes" (vv. 16-17)

Extinguishing Of The Sixth Candle

The Blessing

The Lord's Final Word From The Cross   John 19:30

Solo Meditation   "Jesus, In Thy Dying Woes" (vv. 19, 21)

Extinguishing Of The Seventh Candle

Stripping Of The Altar

The Song   "How Great Thou Art" (vv. 1, 3)
                                                    (#532 LBW)

Removal Of The Christ Candle

The Recessional
   (Please leave the sanctuary silently)

Resources

1. Craddock, Fred, *Overhearing the Gospel* (Nashville, Tennessee: Abingdon Press, 1978), p. 16.

2. Thielicke, Helmut, *Twenty Centuries of Great Preaching* (Waco, Texas: Word Books, Publisher, 1971), vol. 20, p. 269.

3. Bailley, Kenneth E., "The Pursuing Father," pp. 34-40; *Christianity Today*, October 26, 1998.

4. Willimon, William H., *Pulpit Resource* (Inver Grove Heights, Minnesota: Logos Productions Inc., 1998), vol. 26, no. 2, p. 4.